RANELAGH

IN PICTURES

Ranelagh
Arts Festival
2009

RANELAGH

IN PICTURES

A PLACE IN HISTORY

SUSAN ROUNDTREE

British Library Cataloguing in Publication Data
A CIP catalogue record for this book is available from the British Library

ISBN 978-1-906353-12-4

First published in 2009
by
A. & A. Farmar Ltd
78 Ranelagh Village, Dublin 6, Ireland
Tel +353-1-496 3625 e-mail afarmar@iol.ie website www.aafarmar.ie

Printed and bound by GraphyCems
Designed and typeset by Kevin Gurry

PAGE ii A view of the Angle and Field's Terrace c. 1910. *Eason Collection. Courtesy of the National Library of Ireland*

CONTENTS

FOREWORD
Dr Garret FitzGerald

THE IDEA OF publishing a pictorial record of Ranelagh was an excellent one. Accompanied with maps going back to the mid-eighteenth century, and with a number of pre-photographic visual representations, this book spans 250 years of Ranelagh history.

The maps show us the development of the village over that period, as roads were gradually developed on either side of Ranelagh, linking it with Rathmines and Donnybrook. One of these side-roads was Annavilla, where I now live, which was originally an avenue leading up to Anna Villa house itself, but was later extended farther up the hill and linked with what is now Palmerston Road and Upper Rathmines Road. We can also see from the maps the emergence of Ranelagh Gardens, whence early ballooning was launched.

The evolution of the village itself through the whole 150-plus years of photography is set out before us. We can see the emergence of the tramway system, including not only the later-denominated no. 11 tram to Clonskeagh but also an early competing line to Rathmines via Ranelagh, which briefly provided an alternative to what were later numbered the 14 and 15 lines. This Charleston road line was subsequently incorporated into the cross city number 18 route, as a result of which Ranelagh became an important south city tramway junction.

This record shows the emergence of many of Ranelagh's shops over the years, some of which still retain the same shape they had a century or more ago, albeit with changing ownership.

My own memories of Ranelagh go back to 1936 when, with my mother, I travelled on a very bouncy no. 12 tram to Cowper Road, where we looked at a house to which she thought we might need to down-size after our impending departure from our house outside Bray - a move that would probably be necessitated by my father's likely loss of his Dáil seat in Carlow-Kilkenny.

In the event, we spent the next three years in Blackrock before moving to Temple Road, Rathmines where we spent most of the War. Apart from feeding a dozen hens and watering a large number of flowers, every day, my teenage duties included visiting Mrs Scott's shop at the Angle to scrounge as many cigarettes as possible for my father.

In this book, recording much of the history of the village, there is to be found an excellent record of its historic development. I am happy to recommend it to the general public, and particularly the residents of our village!

ACKNOWLEDGEMENTS

This book has been produced with the assistance of many people. I would particularly like to thank Anna and Tony Farmar for suggesting the idea in the first instance and for their professional commitment to making it happen. Special thanks to Sally Corcoran, Rachel McNicholl and Honor O Brolchain for support and sound editorial advice along the way and to Kate Horgan, Daragh Owens and Brigid Tiernan for contributing their wonderful photographs of Ranelagh to complement the older images. Brendan Ellis provided invaluable information on many things to do with Ranelagh and my thanks go to him; also to Ross Galbraith for photography and scanning, and for technical and moral support.

The following people and organisations are gratefully acknowledged for their support and for assistance in procuring images, maps and caption information:

An Post; Angela Bourke; Barry Carse; David Carse; the Ceannt family; Iseult Ní Cléirigh; Michael Corcoran; Sally Corcoran; Margaret Coyle; Brian Crowley; Culwick Choral Society; David Davison; Helen Dillon; Dublin City Council; Dublin City Library & Archive; Colette Edwards; Brendan Ellis; Natasha Evans; Dr Garret FitzGerald; Ross Galbraith; Mary Gallagher; David Griffin; James Connolly Heron; Kate Horgan; Irish Architectural Archive; Catherine Johnson; the late Aidan Kelly; Maire Kennedy; Brian Keighron; Simon Lincoln, the MacDonagh family; Iseult McGuinness; Rachel McNicholl; Justin Martin; Vincent Martin; Gary Morton; Robert Mills; Garry Murphy; Michael Murphy; National Botanic Gardens; National Library of Ireland; the O'Brennan family; Seamus O'Brien; Honor O Brolchain; Anne O'Donnell; Father Eamon O'Donnell; Anne O'Donoghue; Maureen O'Hara; Anne O'Neill; Colum O'Riordan; Daragh Owens; Mrs Betty Owens; Pearse Museum; Royal College of Physicians of Ireland; Sally Ryan; Val Roche; Anne Marie Sheridan; Patrick Shine; Irene Stevenson; the late Michael Stynes; Brigid Tiernan; The Irish Times; The King's Hospital School; Victoria White; Lesley Whiteside.

Finally I would like to acknowledge the generous support for this book from Ranelagh Arts Festival and convey thanks to Terry Connaughton and the festival committee.

A PLACE IN HISTORY
Susan Roundtree

IN 2005 A GROUP of local enthusiasts organised the first Ranelagh Arts Festival. Since then the festival has become a significant fixture each September and continues to deliver on its core objective of creating community links by celebrating the arts. The festival is made possible by a hard-working team of volunteers and by financial and practical support from Dublin City Council, the Arts Council and the local business community.

Over the past four years many different events have contributed to the success of the festival and helped to generate a 'sense of place' in Ranelagh. Residents of all generations have enjoyed exploring the area's local history through walks and talks and guided visits to buildings and gardens. This interest was the motivating factor for the collecting and exhibiting of historic photographs and maps of Ranelagh in Scoil Bhride during the 2007 festival. The exhibition expanded in 2008 as more material came to light or was donated by an increasingly engaged audience. This book contains a selection of the images of people and places drawn from the exhibition. It includes photographs, maps and drawings sourced from both national and private collections.

Ranelagh has very special connections with early photography in Ireland, primarily through the work of Robert French, who lived in Ashfield Avenue and was the main photographer for the Lawrence Collection of over 40,000 images. He was the key figure in the making of this remarkable visual record of the whole of Ireland at the turn of the twentieth century. Another important photographer, Father Browne, who sailed on the maiden voyage of Titantic and whose wonderful photographs were re-discovered in 1985, spent time in Ranelagh when he studied and was ordained for the priesthood at Milltown Park between 1912 and 1916.

Excellent street views of Ranelagh are recorded in photographs from the Eason Collection, created for the Irish postcard trade by Eason & Son between 1900 and 1940. The early black and white scenes of the village are of exceptional quality and clarity. In many respects they show how little has changed in the intervening years, as can be seen when they are matched with contemporary photographs. Some were colour tinted and produced as postcards.

Images of historic trams, trains, buses and cars also feature strongly in this collection as well as some special photographs of individual shops, many sourced locally from private collections. It is, of course, the residents who have shaped Ranelagh, and a selection of the more notable figures are included in this collection - figures past and present who represent, or have represented, Ranelagh at home and on the wider stage – artists, writers, musicians, poets, patriots, explorers, philanthropists and entrepreneurs.

The tradition of photographic recording in Ranelagh continues today with the work of local photographers Kate Horgan, Daragh Owens and Brigid Tiernan, who are all key contributers to the Ranelagh Arts Festival. Their photographs are a critical part of this collection and an important record of Ranelagh and its place in history.

Willbrook and Ranelagh Gardens

The earliest identifiable building in the area we now know as Ranelagh is shown on the John Rocque illustrated map of 1762. Willbrook was, in the early eighteenth century, the home of William Barnard, Bishop of Derry. William Hollister leased the house and grounds in 1768 and opened the venue as the Ranelagh Gardens, named after the gardens of the same name in Chelsea, and for the entertainment of the well-to-do of Dublin. In 1785 Richard Crosbie ascended in a balloon from the gardens. A stamp to commemorate this first flight by an Irishman was issued by An Post in 1985. The house, Willbrook, is clearly visible in the black and white drawing and in the coloured version on the stamp.

OPPOSITE Detail from 'An Actual Survey of the County of Dublin by John Rocque, 1760', showing the Willbrook estate located (roughly in the middle of the map) on the east side of the road from the city to Milltown
Courtesy of Dublin City Council

RIGHT Drawing from the Dixon Collection showing Richard Crosbie's balloon flight
Courtesy of the Gilbert Library

BELOW The First Flight by an Irishman (1785)
Reproduced by kind permission of An Post©

'To be sold to the highest bidder . . . the interest of the lease of Willbrook, held under the See of Dublin . . . containing 6 acres, on which stands a convenient dwelling house . . . with a view of the city, harbour, sea and Wicklow mountains, and a coach house, stables and offices, and a walled garden . . . at the bottom of the garden is a fine canal of a considerable depth stock'd with carp and tench, which is occasionally supplied by a stream of water, and which fronting the house and the lawn opens itself into a large oblong canal, in the middle of which is an island; the parks are remarkably rich, terminating with terraces and canals, and enclosed with hedges and hedgerows, a handsome avenue bounded with a canal leads to the house, the distance from Dublin is one mile on the road leading to Milltown . . .' PUE'S OCCURANCES 24 MAY 1753, NO.24

RICHARD CROSBIE

On 19 January 1785, Wicklow-born
Richard Crosbie (1755–1800) launched his
'Grand Air Balloon and Flying Barge' at
2.30 pm from the Ranelagh Gardens. The
balloon was ornamented with paintings
of Minerva and Mercury supporting the
Arms of Ireland. Crosbie had intended to
cross the Irish Sea but due to early darkness
instead landed safely at Clontarf. This was
a remarkable achievement, occurring just
14 months after the first ever balloon flight,
undertaken by the Montgolfier brothers in
France.

RIGHT A statue to commemorate Richard Crosbie,
by artist Rory Breslin, was unveiled during the 2008
Ranelagh Arts Festival.
Photograph by Daragh Owens

Photographs by Geoff White 1981
Courtesy of the Irish Architectural Archive

THE CARMELITE CONVENT OF ST JOSEPH

Two years after Crosbie's flight the Ranelagh Gardens closed. The Carmelite Order bought Willbrook and came to Ranelagh in 1788. They established a boarding school for girls and later a Poor Law school for local children. The community had a large kitchen garden and the nuns kept poultry and, for a time, their own cattle. The convent survived there until 1975 when the lands were sold and the remaining community moved to Malahide. The house was subsequently demolished and the lands developed for housing. A section of the land to the south of the house was transferred to Dublin Corporation and is now a public park, retaining the original name of Ranelagh Gardens.

These images of the former convent building were taken in 1981 and show the original house as depicted in the etching of the Richard Crosbie balloon flight. The photographs show elements of its fine early Georgian interior—the staircase hall and an example of an early window shuttercase.

OLD MOUNTPLEASANT

Opposite the entrance to Ranelagh Gardens, and behind the Ranelagh Multi-denominational School, stands one of the oldest terraces of houses in the area, Old Mountpleasant. These houses date from the last decades of the eighteenth century. The earliest house, no. 6, shown above, once stood on its own, and was home to the architect Thomas Ivory in the 1770s. Ivory was a most important figure in Irish architecture at this time. He was both a teacher of drawing and a talented building designer. His Dublin buildings include the original Bluecoat School (now the Law Society Headquarters in Blackhall Place) and Newcomen Bank on Cork Hill (now the Dublin City Council Rates Office), both considered among the finest examples of eighteenth-century architecture in the city.

Photograph by Susan Roundtree

THOMAS IVORY

The architect Thomas Ivory, who designed the Bluecoat School, lived in Old Mountpleasant (opposite). This painting by John Trotter c.1773 shows Thomas Ivory (centre) with the other eighteenth-century planners of the Bluecoat School. Simon Vierpyl, the master stonecutter, is seated to the right of Ivory.

Courtesy of the Governors of The King's Hospital

MOUNTPLEASANT SQUARE

Mountpleasant Square is an important late-Georgian residential development constructed between 1803 and 1830. The central park, now largely occupied by Mountpleasant Lawn Tennis Club, is enclosed by curved terraces north and south, with a straight terrace to the west. Unusually for this period, the square was laid out and built largely by one developer, Terence Dolan, who had started out life as a glove maker. His son, Terence T. Dolan, was one of the founding commissioners of the Rathmines Township 1847.

The Swan River, although now in culvert and entirely hidden from view, was once an important natural feature in the Ranelagh area and, in the case of Mountpleasant, influenced how the layout of the square evolved. Coming from Rathmines, it crosses the central park from west to east, crosses the main road and then traverses Ranelagh Gardens, finding its way eventually to join the Dodder River near Ballsbridge.

Photographs by Susan Roundtree

OPPOSITE Mountpleasant Square c.1870
Ordnance Survey, Dublin, Sheet 18.XV
Courtesy of OSi and Dublin City Council

CULLENSWOOD HOUSE

Another survivor from the eighteenth century is Cullenswood House on Oakley Road (formerly called Cullenswood Avenue). This house has played a very important role in the history of the area. In 1908 it became home to Patrick Pearse's school, St Enda's. Two years later the school moved to Rathfarnham and Cullenswood House became a bilingual school for girls, St Ita's, until 1912. The tradition of education continues at the house today with Gaelscoil Lios na nÓg installed in the extended and restored house beside Scoil Bhríde.

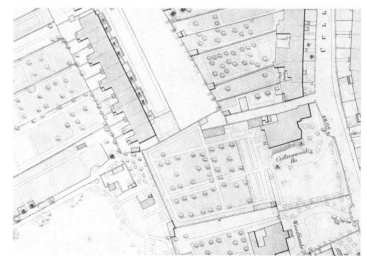

Centenary of the opening of St Enda's by Patrick Pearse

On 25 September 2008, An Post issued two stamps
to commemorate the centenary of the opening of St
Enda's by Patrick Pearse. The school was established
as a 'brave attempt' to reform and regenerate Irish
education by providing a wide curriculum, four
or five modern languages and a combination of
practical skills and academic learning with outdoor
games and activities. The stamps are based on
original illustrations by Thomas Ryan RHA and
feature portraits of Patrick Pearse in the foreground
with the buildings which housed St Enda's over the
years in the background.
Reproduced by kind permission of An Post©

BROOKVILLE, SALLYMOUNT AVENUE

Patrick Pearse's first school was in the family house in
Ranelagh at Brookville, 17 Sallymount Avenue (now
demolished).

Drawing from the Irish Press, *9 April 1966*

PATRICK PEARSE

Born in 1879, in Great Brunswick Street, now Pearse
Street, in Dublin. Patrick Pearse was educated at the
Christian Brothers School, Westland Row, and then
at the Royal University, studying arts and law before
being called to the Bar. He decided to set up his own
school based on the principle that an Irish school
must have Irish culture, the repository of which is the
Irish language. His first school was in the family house
in Ranelagh at Brookville, 17 Sallymount Avenue.
In 1908, St Enda's, a much bigger venture, opened
its doors at Cullenswood House on Oakley Road
where he and his family also lived. Pearse's ideas on
education were advanced, humane and international.
He read and admired Maria Montessori and, like her,
believed that education is an agent for social change,
that the child is paramount, and that the school is
for the child's physical, recreational, aesthetic, moral
and cultural development. St Enda's later moved to
Rathfarnham.

Pearse joined the Gaelic League in 1895. He
became editor of its paper, *An Claidheamh Soluis*. He
wrote stories, essays and poems in Irish and English
and was a contributor to many literary journals.
Initially a supporter of Home Rule, he joined the Irish
Republican Brotherhood (IRB) in 1913, was co-opted
to its supreme council and elected to the Volunteers'
committee. In the 1916 Rising he was Commandant-
General of the Army of the Irish Republic and
President of the Provisional Government, spending
the week in the GPO headquarters until fires drove
him, and more than 300 men and women, out onto
Moore Street, eventually to surrender unconditionally
to prevent the further slaughter of civilians. Patrick
Pearse was executed on 3 May 1916.

WILLIE AND PATRICK PEARSE

Close friends all their lives. Willie and Patrick Pearse shared in many things from teaching, to running St Enda's, to the Rising in the GPO and Moore Street, where Willie was a leader of the surrendering troops, to Parnell Square and on to Richmond Barracks and Kilmainham Gaol where, thanks to his jailers, he just missed seeing Patrick before he was shot. He was executed the day after his brother, Patrick, on 4 May 1916.

Photograph by kind permission of Brian Crowley and the Pearse Museum, St Enda's, Rathfarnham

ÁINE CEANNT

Widow of the executed 1916 leader, Éamonn Ceannt, she was born Frances (Fanny) O'Brennan in Dublin in 1880. She and her sisters were educated in the Dominican Convent, Eccles Street. On leaving school, she joined the Gaelic League and Cumann na bPíobairí (the Pipers Club) and through them she met Éamonn Ceannt. They married in 1905 and she later changed her name to Áine. Their son, Ronan, was born in 1906. Áine had joined Cumann na mBan in 1914 and, after Éamonn's execution in 1916, served as Vice-President and member of the Standing Committee until 1925. In 1918, she and her family moved from Dolphin's Barn to 44 Oakley Road (Baerendorf). She was elected to Rathmines Urban District Council where she served as Vice-Chairman. In 1920–21 she acted as a District Justice in the Rathmines and Rathgar Dáil Éireann courts and as an arbitrator in wage disputes. Her home in Oakley Road, raided on several occasions, often sheltered men on the run, elected Dáil members having to leave in a hurry, even in their pyjamas. She was a founder of the Irish White Cross, which worked on behalf of child victims of the troubles in Ireland. She served as honorary treasurer of the Irish Red Cross until 1947. She died in 1954 and is buried in Deansgrange.

Photograph by kind permission of Mary Gallagher and the O'Brennan and Ceannt families

ÉAMONN CEANNT

His family moved to Dublin from Galway in 1891 when he was ten. He went to the Christian Brothers School, North Richmond Street, and then joined Dublin Corporation where he worked in the City Treasurer's Office. Through the Gaelic League and Irish music (he played the uileann pipes) he met the other leaders of the 1916 Rising and joined the Irish Republican Brotherhood (IRB). He was a founder member of the Volunteers and a key figure in the Howth gunrunning. He became a member of the Military Council of the IRB which often met in his house at 2 Dolphin Terrace, Dolphin's Barn, and from early on he was deeply involved in the plans for the Rising. In Easter Week 1916, he was in command of the 4th Battalion at the South Dublin Union (where St James's Hospital now stands). He was executed in Kilmainham Gaol on 8 May, 1916.

Photograph courtesy of the National Library of Ireland

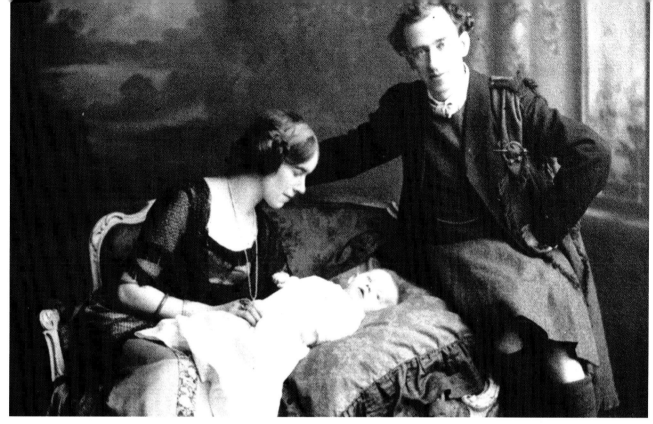

Thomas MacDonagh

The son of two teachers, Thomas MacDonagh was born in Cloughjordan, Co. Tipperary, in 1878. He was educated at Rockwell College and at University College Dublin (UCD). He taught in Kilkenny, Fermoy and, from 1908, in St Enda's, on Oakley Road in Ranelagh. In 1912, a few months after their marriage in the Church of the Holy Name, Beechwood Avenue, Thomas and Muriel MacDonagh (née Gifford) moved to 29 Oakley Road, where Donagh and, two years later, Bairbre, were born. Thomas was an imaginative and lyrical poet, involved in many literary journals and publications including *The Irish Review*. He was co-founder of the Irish Theatre with Joseph Plunkett and Edward Martyn. As a lecturer in University College Dublin, he was a witness to police brutality in 1913 and became involved in the founding of the Volunteers. He was a major figure at the Howth gunrunning and, in 1915, the organiser of the O'Donovan Rossa funeral. Some months later he became a member of the Military Council for the 1916 Rising. He commanded the 2nd Battalion at Jacob's Factory in Easter Week, 1916. A message was sent to his wife in Oakley Road that she could see him before he was shot but Muriel did not have the requisite pass so she could not get through the military cordons to the jail. Thomas MacDonagh was executed on 3 May, 1916. Muriel was drowned in a bathing accident a year later.

ABOVE Thomas, Muriel and Donagh MacDonagh, 1912   *Photograph by kind permission of Iseult McGuinness and the descendants of those in the photograph*

ABOVE The Carse family house on Oakley Road

Photograph by Susan Roundtree

Samuel Barry Carse

The editor of Thom's *Directory* from 1907 until 1955, Samuel Carse lived in Oakley Road. This photograph shows him at home with his daughter-in-law, Elizabeth, and grandson, Barry. In 1916, during the Rising, Thom's works in Abbey Street were burned and reduced to ashes and all the standing type was destroyed. Mr Carse set to work, buying or borrowing copies of the previous year's directory. He got every page re-set and corrected and the new edition ready by March 1917—an extraordinary feat. His son, Samuel Joseph Carse, also worked with Thom's and his grandsons, Barry and David, still live on Oakley Road.

Photograph courtesy of David Carse

MARY HOLLAND

Another important resident on Oakley Road, Mary Holland was an outstanding journalist who covered the troubles in Northern Ireland over three decades, writing for *The Irish Times* and the *Observer*, among other publications. Her work was distinguished by its integrity and humanity, and as a result she had access to, and respect from, all parties in the conflict. Her analysis of the problems in Northern Ireland was significant both in the development of informed public opinion and in securing attention at both government and parliamentary level. She will also be remembered for her contributions to civil rights and the trade union movement. She had two children, Kitty and Luke. She died in June 2004.

Photograph courtesy of The Irish Times

Dr Kathleen Lynn

Born in Mayo in 1874, she received her medical degree from the Royal University and was the first female resident at the Royal Victoria Eye and Ear Hospital, Dublin. In 1904 she set up general practice at 9 Belgrave Road, with particular benefit to the poor of the area. In the 1913 Lockout she gave support and aid to the workers and joined the Irish Citizen Army as Captain and Chief Medical Officer. She was in the garrison at City Hall during the 1916 Rising. She was imprisoned in Mountjoy Jail and exiled to England. When she returned to Ireland no hospital would employ her. Elected to the Sinn Féin executive in 1917, she attended the wounded during the War of Independence. She made her house calls in disguise and her house was repeatedly raided. Arrested in 1918, she was released to help treat victims of the 1918 'flu epidemic.

In 1919 she and her great friend Madeleine ffrench-Mullen, who lived with Dr Lynn in 9 Belgrave Road for 30 years until her death in 1944, established Ireland's first infant hospital, St Ultan's, Charlemont Street. Though elected to the Dáil, Kathleen Lynn did not take her seat as she was anti-Treaty. She was elected to the Rathmines Urban District Council where she served until 1930. She worked until she died in 1955 and was buried with full military honours.

LEFT Dr Kathleen Lynn and Madeleine ffrench-Mullen, c.1919
Courtesy of the Royal College of Physicians of Ireland

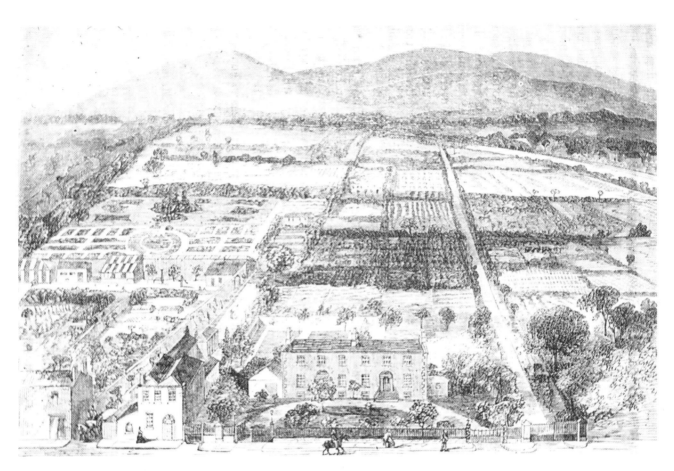

TOOLE'S NURSERIES

Toole's Nurseries were founded in 1777 by Charles and Luke Toole. The nurseries covered a large area of present-day Ranelagh from Mornington Road to Beechwood Road and across to Elmwood Avenue. This drawing is an aerial view of the nurseries dating from about 1850. The two houses in the foreground still exist behind the Ulster Bank at the bottom of Lower Beechwood Avenue, described as Elm Grove on the map overleaf. The layout and extent of the nurseries is also seen on the 1870s Ordnance Survey map on p.20. Toole's Nurseries closed towards the end of the nineteenth century as the value of land for building in Ranelagh rose. The nurseries specialised in trees and supplied them to various demesnes, such as Powerscourt, and also to the Botanic Gardens. Stephen Mackey was a partner in Toole's in the nineteenth century and Mackey's were still in the nursery and plant supply business until very recently.

Drawing from the Dixon Collection
Courtesy of the Gilbert Library

THIS PAGE Cullenswood Lodge, no. 130 Ranelagh
Photograph courtesy of the Irish Architectural Archive

OPPOSITE Ranelagh c.1870 Ordnance Survey, Dublin, Sheet 18.XV, c.1870
Courtesy of OSi and Dublin City Council

CULLENSWOOD LODGE

The road travelling south from the city through present-day Ranelagh follows the same alignment as that shown on the 1870s map. Development along the route was, however, still in the form of two separate villages at that date. Ranelagh Road is the section from Charlemont Bridge to the newly-created Angle; Cullenswood Road from there to the junction with Bushfield Avenue (now Marlborough Road); and Sandford Road to the junction with Belmont Avenue. The townland names from north to south are Ranelagh North, Ranelagh South, Sallymount and Cullenswood. Cullenswood Lodge, shown in this photograph (now demolished) was an interesting early house located on the main road close to Cullenswood Park.

Early twentieth-century views of Ranelagh

The following photographs from the Eason Collection are undated but the shop names agree with those contained in the street directories of c.1910.

A view from the end of Lower Beechwood Avenue looking towards the Angle, with Chelmsford Road on the right and Elmpark Avenue on the left. The scene is instantly recognisable except for the absence of traffic (note the tram tracks and the overhead tram lines). The boy in the sailor suit is outside the Singer sewing machine shop in the terrace that was then known as Elm Park Villas.

Eason Collection
Courtesy of the National Library of Ireland

A view of Ranelagh looking towards the Angle from the bottom of Elmpark Avenue; 'E. Field Cab and Car Proprietors' is written over the arched doorway on the right. Opposite stands a waiting cab at the Angle, still the place to find a taxi cab in Ranelagh today.

Eason Collection
Courtesy of the National Library of Ireland

A view of the shops on what was then called Macgowan Terrace. Gordon's hardware shop, with its wonderful window displays and signage, stands on the corner now occupied by the Centra shop. The Dublin Laundry Co. Ltd and the Dartry Dye Works Ltd are next in the terrace, then J. & H. Memery, family grocers, McCabe's, and then Johnston's Pharmacy, now Burke's.

Eason Collection
Courtesy of the National Library of Ireland

Little has changed in the overall form of this terrace in this 1990s photograph
taken before the construction of the new Luas station.

Photograph courtesy of Garry Murphy

A view looking at the terrace opposite Gordon's: W. & A . Gilbey Ltd, Branch Depot, stood on the corner of Ranelagh Avenue on the site now occupied by the forecourt of the AIB. Gordon's Medical Hall was next door, then an amazing display of meat carcasses outside Pendred's.

Eason Collection
Courtesy of the National Library of Ireland

A view of the terrace opposite the Angle shows the Lucan Dairy, Lyster & Sons, and Barretts at no. 33, on the corner of Ranelagh Avenue. This terrace was demolished and rebuilt; it is now occupied by The Ranelagh Collection and Diep At Home.

Eason Collection
Courtesy of the National Library of Ireland

A view of the Angle and Field's Terrace showing the waiting cabs and cab drivers
and the Chester Dairy beside Gordon's, then the home of the Ranelagh Post Office,
as Centra is today. The Angle itself appears to have been enclosed by railings at this
time.

Eason Collection
Courtesy of the National Library of Ireland

A photograph of the Angle taken in 2007 shows that the buildings have changed little, though the signage and road plan are notably different.

Photograph by Daragh Owens

ROBERT FRENCH

Working for the Dublin photographic firm of William Lawrence, he started as a printer and worked his way up to chief photographer. He was the main photographer for the Lawrence Collection, consisting of over 40,000 plates, acquired by the National Library of Ireland in 1943. These wonderful photographs depict scenes of life in the cities and towns and throughout the country. The collection is a remarkable visual record of the whole of Ireland at the turn of the twentieth century.

Robert French was born in Dublin in 1841, the eldest of seven children born to William French, a court messenger, and Ellen Johnson. At nineteen he joined the Royal Irish Constabulary and was posted to the barracks in Glenealy, Co. Wicklow. While stationed there he met his future wife, Henrietta Jones, from nearby Newcastle. He resigned from the Constabulary in 1862 and returned to Dublin to take up a position of printer in the photographic studio of William Lawrence. He married Henrietta in 1863. By 1869 he is described as an 'artist'; three years later as an assistant photographer. He was subsequently put in charge of Lawrence's outdoor photographic work such as the photograph of Palmerstown Park on page 32. He photographed town life, landscapes, railways, shipping, transport, churches, ruins, hotels, public buildings, statues, banks, military activities, golfing, fairs and markets, tourists and tourism, as well as the occasional posed picture.

He retired in 1914 and died on 24 June in 1917, having lived to see O'Connell Street and the Lawrence studio that had spawned his extraordinary career, in ruins after the events of Easter 1916.

OPPOSITE Robert French at retirement c.1914
Courtesy of the National Library of Ireland

ABOVE 13 Ashfield Avenue, home of Robert French
Photograph by Susan Roundtree

PALMERSTON PARK

A fine photograph of Palmerston Park by Robert French, the chief photographer of the Lawrence Collection, who lived in Ranelagh at Ashfield Avenue.

THE CHURCH OF THE HOLY NAME (CATHOLIC)

The Parish of the Holy Name, Cullenswood, was established in 1906, as a separate parish from Rathgar. Construction of the church began a year later. It was designed by Dublin architects William H. Byrne & Son and formally opened on 28 June 1914. The neighbourhood was in a sense an isolated one, cut off behind the main Sandford Road and the railway line, but it was a popular residential area. The church was, and remains today, a striking landmark in the area, with its dramatic tower and belfry. The church has an elaborate interior decorated with marble and mosaic and many fine stained glass windows. In this early photograph the building appears to be newly complete although without its boundary railings. Just visible to the left is the old tin chapel of ease which it replaced.

Eason Collection
Courtesy of the National Library of Ireland

MAUREEN O'HARA

The Hollywood film star was born on 17 August 1920, and spent her childhood at 32 Upper Beechwood Avenue, close to the Church of the Holy Name. She was the second of six children. At the time of her birth, her father, Charles Fitzsimons, owned a shop on the Angle. He was also a part-owner of the famous Shamrock Rovers Football Club. Maureen excelled at sports and had a natural talent for performing. She joined the Abbey Theatre and was still a teenager when, in 1939, she was brought to Hollywood by the English actor Charles Laughton to star in *The Hunchback of Notre Dame*. She starred in many film classics with some of Hollywood's most famous leading men and worked with some of the greatest directors in the movie business. She retired from the film industry in 1973 to manage a commuter sea plane service with her husband, Charles Blair, in the Caribbean. Tragically, her husband died in a plane crash in 1978. She is now semi-retired and living in the Virgin Islands.

Photographs courtesy of Maureen O'Hara

THE HARCOURT STREET RAILWAY LINE

The double-track suburban railway, popularly known as the Harcourt Street Line, opened in 1854 from Harcourt Street station to serve the expanding southern suburbs, eventually travelling through Dundrum and Foxrock to Bray.

The bridge at Charleston Road, Ranelagh, 1953.

O'Dea Collection
Courtesy of the National Library of Ireland

The Rathmines & Ranelagh station on the Harcourt Street Line at Dunville Avenue opened in 1896. A decision to close the line was taken in 1958. Forty years later, in May 1998, the Government decided to invest in a new light railway system and the Luas green line to Sandyford opened in 2004 on the same alignment as the original line.

O'Dea Collection
Courtesy of the National Library of Ireland

Class J15 no. 188 with a Harcourt Street to Bray train at Rathmines & Ranelagh station (now Beechwood Luas station) c.1955.

Photograph courtesy of David Carse

The railway bridge at Dunville Avenue in the 1950s, with the entrance to the Rathmines & Ranelagh station under the bridge on the right.

O'Dea Collection
Courtesy of the National Library of Ireland

Dismantling the railway bridge at Ranelagh Road in the late 1950s; it was subsequently replaced by the Luas bridge and Ranelagh station.

O'Dea Collection
Courtesy of the National Library of Ireland

THE LOCAL TRAM

The No. 11 bus took over the tram route.

Image courtesy of Michael Corcoran

THE HARCOURT STREET LINE REVIVED
The first Luas tram arriving at Beechwood on 30 June 2004 .

Photographs by Kate Horgan

POSTCARD VIEWS OF RANELAGH

Ranelagh Road, c.1910

Postcard courtesy of Brian Keighron

The Angle, Ranelagh, c.1910, with the characteristic Dublin 'outside cars' waiting for hire.

Postcard courtesy of Brian Keighron

Ranelagh, Dublin.

Ranelagh, c.1910. Looking south, on the left Lucan Dairy, where Diep At Home is now, facing the Angle. Evidence of trams, bicycles and various horse-drawn vehicles, but no motor-cars as yet.

Postcard courtesy of Brian Keighron

Sandford Road, Ranelagh, Dublin

Ranelagh, looking towards Sandford Road, 1950s. Scarcely more traffic than 40 years before. The terrace on the left dates from the 1840s and now contains the office of this book's publishers.

Dixon Collection
Courtesy of the Gilbert Library

Ranelagh Road, 1950s, looking south from the railway bridge.

Postcard courtesy of Brian Keighron

Ranelagh, 2007, looking south from the same vantage point with the brand-new Ranelagh Luas station on the right.

Photograph by Daragh Owens

DEIRDRE KELLY

Historian, conservationist and friend of Dublin and its people, Deirdre was a founding member of the Living City group and was involved in many campaigns to save Dublin's architectural and social heritage, including Hume Street and Wood Quay. She was born in 1938 in Upper Leeson Street, later moving to Ranelagh, where she lived at Old Mountpleasant with her husband Aidan and their four children–Maeve, Diarmuid, Mahon and Hugh. She attended the National College of Art as a student, worked as an artist in the National Museum of Ireland and as a teacher of art at Inchicore Vocational School. As a mature student she studied history and archaeology at University College Dublin. She had a great passion for local history and was a founding member of the Ranelagh, Rathmines and Rathgar Historical Society. She spent her life investigating and researching this part of Dublin and delving into archives to discover the history of the area. Her research culminated in the publication of the definitive history of the Ranelagh, Rathmines and Leeson Street area, *Four Roads to Dublin*, in 1995. A memorial to Deirdre Kelly, who died in 2000, was installed at the Angle in February 2009.

'Wherever one walks one is conscious that these are living streets steeped not just in their own history but woven into the history of Dublin. Writers and musicians, unionists and nationalists, scientists, poets and artists lived—and still do—in the houses which line the streets.'

Photograph courtesy of the Kelly family

THE ANGLE, RANELAGH IN 2003

Photograph by Garry Murphy

Ranelagh from Sandford Road looking north, c. 1910; the terrace on the left survives. Harrison's (now the Gourmet Burger) was then a wholesale and retail tobacconist (one of several in the village) selling Havana cigars and willing to deliver morning and evening papers to any address. The wonderful 'sugar stick' lamp standard opposite is a very early design; only a few examples of this type can be found in Ranelagh today.

Eason Collection
Courtesy of the National Library of Ireland

SANDFORD CHURCH. RECTORY. 7639. W.L.

SANDFORD RECTORY

The rectory for Sandford Parish is immediately to the south of the church and is little changed from this Lawrence Collection photograph. The architectural style of the house is very similar to that of Sandford Park (1894) and the terrace of houses in the Arts & Crafts style built on Sandford Road by James Pile in the first decade of the twentieth century.

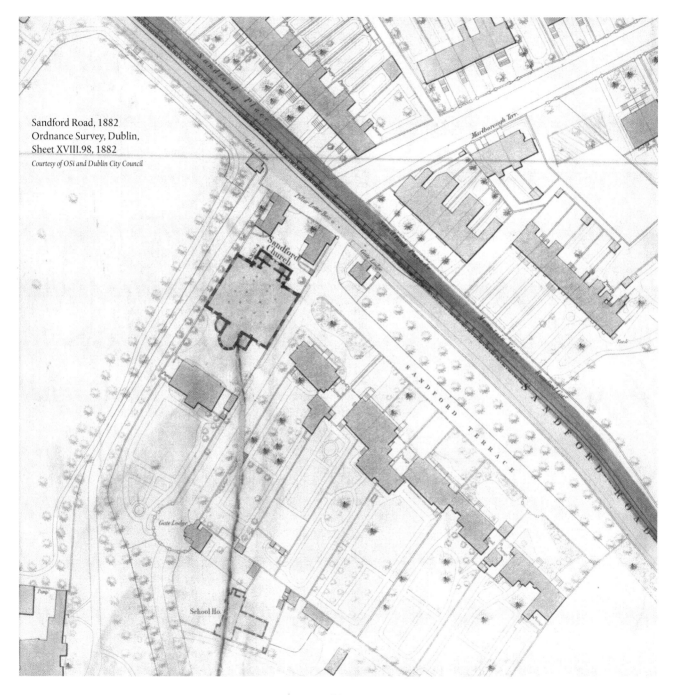

Sandford Road, 1882
Ordnance Survey, Dublin,
Sheet XVIII.98, 1882

Courtesy of OSi and Dublin City Council

Sandford Church, Ranelagh, Dublin

SANDFORD PARISH CHURCH (CHURCH OF IRELAND)

Sandford Church was originally a chapel-of-ease to St Peter's Church in Aungier Street. The church was erected by Robert Newenham, who lived in Merton House. George Baron Mountsandford provided the site and the money for the chapel and school. The original church was opened on 26 June 1826. It was a plain building, flanked by two cottages (as can be seen on the early Ordnance Survey map opposite). Sandford became a parish in its own right in 1858. The façade was rebuilt in granite masonry in 1860 to a design by the eminent architects Lanyon, Lynn and Lanyon of Belfast. In 1880 the side aisles and chancel apse were added. A remarkable stained glass window by Harry Clarke, with two lights depicting St Peter and St Paul, from 1921, is a highlight of the interior. The church gave its name to the road to Milltown, which built up from 1860 to 1900.

Sandford Church c.1910

Courtesy of Michael Murphy

Augustine,
Elsie

Sir Jocelyn Gore Boot

AUGUSTINE HENRY
1857–1930

Augustine Henry was a plantsman and sinologist who lived at no. 5 Sandford Terrace (now no. 47 Sandford Road) from 1913 until his death in 1930. He entered the Imperial Customs Service in Shanghai in 1881 as Assistant Medical Officer and Customs Assistant. He was sent to the remote posting of Yichang (Ichang) in Central China in 1882 to investigate plants used in Chinese medicine. He collected plants, seeds and specimens, many not previously known, and sent over 158,000 dry specimens and seeds and 1,700 plant samples to Kew Gardens. In 1888 he published a list of Chinese plants for the *Journal of the Royal Asiatic Society*. On his return to Europe he spent some time working at Kew Gardens. He was joint author with Henry John Elwes of the seven-volume *Trees of Great Britain and Ireland*, 1907–13. In 1913 he took up the Chair of Forestry at the Royal College of Science (later University College Dublin) and is known internationally as the founding father of Irish forestry.

ABOVE Augustine Henry 1929
Courtesy of the library at the National Botanic Gardens, Glasnevin, Dublin 9

OPPOSITE Augustine and Elsie Henry with Sir Jocelyn Gore-Booth at Lissadell c.1920
Courtesy of the National Library of Ireland

THE DILLON GARDEN

Helen Dillon 's famous town garden at no. 45 Sandford Road, is set around a reflective canal edged with Irish limestone. The mixed borders of shrubs and herbaceous perennials are full of unusual plants and feature exciting colour combinations, including rarities such as lady's slipper orchids, or double-flowered *Trillium*, and *Lilium Henryi*, named after Augustine Henry, who had lived next door. Terracotta pots on a sunken terrace sprout more rare plants. Clumps of angel's fishing rods arch over sphinxes, and a small alpine house and conservatory shelter the choicest species, including what is considered to be the most beautiful climber in the world—the national flower of Chile, *Lapageria rosea*. The Dillon Garden is open to the public at selected times during the spring and summer months.

Photographs by Susan Roundtree

FATHER BROWNE

Father Francis Browne SJ was born in Cork in 1880 and went to school in Athlone and Dublin. At the age of seventeen he went on a tour of Europe with his brother and his camera and developed his initial interest in photography. He joined the Jesuits and later studied philosophy for three years near Turin. From 1906 to 1911, he taught Latin and Greek at Belvedere College, Dublin, where he founded the Camera Club. From 1912 to 1916, he studied theology in Milltown Park, Ranelagh and was ordained a priest in 1915. He served as Chaplain to the Irish Guards with whom he served on the Somme and at Ypres. He returned to Dublin in 1920 and resumed his teaching career at Belvedere.

He was involved in the organisation of a major photographic event, the first Irish Salon of Photography in Dublin's Civic Week of 1927. Such was the success of this event that further Salons were held every second year until the outbreak of World War II. He continued to take photographs for the rest of his life and, at the time of his death in 1960, had accumulated a collection of 42,000 negatives, all neatly captioned and dated. These negatives were discovered in a trunk by E. E. O'Donnell SJ in the Jesuit archives in Dublin during 1985. He arranged for them to be transferred to safety-film and to be catalogued. Nearly 35,000 photographs in the collection were taken in Ireland and, of these just over 4,600 were taken in Dublin—the earliest in 1906 and the last in 1958 at Gonzaga College, Sandford Road.

RIGHT Portrait of Father Browne, taken in 1939 by his fellow-Jesuit, Michael Garahy
Courtesy of Davison & Associates

SANDFORD HILL AND SANDFORD GROVE

Two fine early nineteenth-century houses that were originally part of the Bewley Estate. They were acquired by the Jesuits in 1949 and are now part of the Gonzaga College buildings.

Photographs by Susan Roundtree

Maeve Brennan

Maeve Brennan, short story writer and staff member of *The New Yorker*, spent her childhood in Ranelagh, first in Belgrave Road, then in no. 48 Cherryfield Avenue. The area is a strong presence in many of her short stories. Both her father, Robert Brennan, and her mother Una Bolger, were active in the War of Independence and Robert was on the run at various times during Maeve's childhood. He took the Republican side in the Civil War and the family suffered economic hardship. In 1934, when Maeve was seventeen, her father was posted to Washington DC as part of the Irish diplomatic corps and the family settled in the USA for a number of years. In 1949, Maeve joined the staff of *The New Yorker*, to which she contributed for more than thirty years. Between 1954 and 1981, she wrote for 'The Talk of the Town' column, a series of sketches about life in Manhattan, which she later compiled into a book called *The Long-Winded Lady* (1969). Collections of her short stories were published over the years, the most recent being the posthumous *The Springs of Affection* (1997). Also after her death in 1993, an unknown novella, written in the mid 1940s, was discovered and published in 2001 as *The Visitor*, to great critical acclaim. In 2004, another resident of Cherryfield Avenue, the distinguished academic Angela Bourke, published a biography of Maeve Brennan, under the title *Maeve Brennan: Homesick at* The New Yorker.

LEFT Portrait of Maeve Brennan in New York 1948
Courtesy of the family of Karl Bissinger (photographer)

JAMES CULWICK

James Culwick (1845–1907) came to Ireland in 1866 to take up a position as church organist in Parsontown, now Birr, Co. Offaly. In 1868, he became organist in Bray, later moving to St Ann's in Dawson Street. In 1881, he became organist and choirmaster to the Chapel Royal in Dublin Castle, where he remained for the rest of his life. He was also Professor of Pianoforte and Theory at Alexandra College for 27 years. From the outset, he was both an industrious academic and an activist with a mission to communicate his own passion for music, particularly indigenous Irish music, to as wide and varied an audience as possible.

In 1898, he founded the Orpheus Choral Society and threw himself with enthusiasm into the Celtic Revival of music and literature, becoming a founder member of the Feis Ceoil. He had one son, Arthur, from his first marriage, and a daughter, Florence, from his second marriage to Mary Richardson. The family lived at 28 Leeson Park for many years. After his death in 1907, Florence continued her father's choir work and, in 1913, the re-formed mixed choir became 'Miss Culwick's Choral Society', subsequently 'The Culwick Choral Society'. A list of the various conductors reads like a *Who's Who* of music, including names such as Alice Yoakley, Joseph Groocock, Seoirse Bodley, Eric Sweeney, Colin Mawby and Colin Block. The Culwick Choral Society continues to perform the traditional works of the great performers as well as experimenting with new music.

Photograph courtesy of the Culwick Choral Society

Memories of Ranelagh
Brendan Ellis

THE EMOTIONAL CENTRE of Ranelagh was undoubtedly Morelli's chip shop (now Antica Venezia) on Ashfield Road where young lust and confusion mixed with Pepsi and the smell of fish and chips, the sounds of the juke box and the scrape of names being etched into the wooden booths at which we were not quite sitting, keeping our options open. And dancing in Percy's on Belmont Avenue, or Mountpleasant Lawn Tennis Club; it never occurred to me to play tennis in either place, although I'm sure there were people who did.

There was a dance hall in the village, too, in Chelmsford Lane, the Ranelagh Boxing and Social Club, intended to keep the kids from the now demolished Mountpleasant Buildings off the streets and out of trouble, and where there was sometimes a confusion as to whether any given night was a boxing night or a dancing night, but it produced good boxers and dancers either way. Further down that lane was Mr Gray's yard with its pigs and horses, and old Mr Jacobs's tumbledown shed, a treasure trove of bits and bobs beside the boxing club, and at the end of the lane where it emerged onto Sallymount Avenue, the Pearses' home crumbling about the heads of the occupants, ignored by all.

Mr Scully the jeweller lived in one of the last two occupied cottages in the lane. He had a little shop on Ranelagh, 96A, where the barbers now is, next to Lily's Dairy, where Boylesports and the Sandford Gallery are now, and the corner shop where O'Brien shoe repairs kept us happy reading comics aloud, listening to stories from old Mr O'Brien, and relaxing in the smell of leather and solvents. Mr O'Brien's young apprentice was Tom O'Neill who later opened his own shop across Sallymount, in the office of Walton's funeral undertakers and car hire company. Later on he moved to Dunville Avenue as O'Neill's Fashion Shoe Repairs where he remained until his recent sudden death.

Lily's Dairy was owned by a family named O'Sullivan (the painter Donal O'Sullivan was a son); there were several other O'Sullivan grocery shops in Ranelagh but I have no idea if they were related: Nora O'Sullivan and Con O'Sullivan on each side of what became the Morris Minor Centre—that too now gone—and Bridget O'Sullivan of the Boyne Stores at the Triangle, where the jewellers was, Con O'Sullivan's was where the Ranelagh Arts Festival shop is now, and there were three Martins, who were related—brothers, I think; one had a shop where the Black Tie is—his son is Phillip Martin, the pianist; one had a hairdresser's where Diep At Home now is and Luigi's used to be and the third kept a serious tobacconist's down at the Triangle where an affected young man could buy Balkan Sobranie cigarettes. (The Gem cycle shop on Chelmsford Road was owned by another Martin altogether.)

Around the corner on Ranelagh was a less serious tobacconist's, Ryan's, where you could buy Peggy's Leg and clay pipes for 4d which was the price of a packet of Tayto or a small bottle of red lemonade (plus 2d back on the bottle) and was the price of admission into the Sandford Cinema on Saturday afternoon, after queuing in Collier's Lane, being terrorised by a power-mad and uniformed usher. But Ryan's frivolous front belied its reality—it was the Ranelagh Billiard Rooms and slipping through the narrow entrance hallway into the back, you'd find an unbelievably romantic place in black and white with smoke hanging in the air and the clack of the billiard balls and the trains passing on the embankment at the back, and the voice from above growling, 'What are you doing in here gettout.' I never went there as an adult so I can't check my memory of it. It's gone now, of course.

Right at the beginning of Ranelagh, or where we thought of Ranelagh as beginning, after the great curve on Ranelagh Road past Mountpleasant and the Tin Church and the Turkish baths, was the grim, forbidding entrance under the railway to the Convent, gates almost always closed and with strange magical symbols carved ominously into the stone to give you pause as you slipped in past the lodge whose keeper might eat you, then hare it across the grounds and out over the wall into Chelmsford Avenue.

The railway station in Ranelagh was where the Beechwood Luas stop is now and the next stop was the terminus at Harcourt Street in that wonderful building where the Odeon bar is and where, in 1904, on 14 February the train didn't quite stop and came out onto Hatch Street.

We would go out of our way to get the train to school, walk up Beechwood Avenue and pay the penny for the single stop and walk, already late, under the great railway bridge over Harcourt Road with its prison-like stores beneath, with steel barred gates and water dripping darkly down the stones, to Gavan Duffy's school in Earlsfort Terrace, or around the corner into Camden Street, to the school in Grantham Street. The railway bridge in Ranelagh, though much smaller, had something of that darkness, a gateway into the Shangri-La of Ranelagh; Dowling's shoe repairs, where the O'Reillys lived and where old Mrs O'Reilly used call on 'the mother o' petrol sucker' for help; McCarthy's, the Ranelagh Shoe Shop, still there, shod generations of us and always at a good price; Considine's hairdressers, where the Village Barbers is; Daly's bicycle shop; the Slobber Maher's, where Superquinn's is, roughly, and Gilbey's Wine & Spirits. And on the other side, the Arch Market; and, in black perspex and aluminium, the Launderette, which introduced many of the flat dwellers to the idea of clean clothes not cleaned by The Mammy. Johnston's Pharmacy, where Mr Wilson would provide medical treatment and perform minor surgery, has morphed into Burke's. Redmond's is still there too, of course, but now no longer a grocer's as well. You could buy your whole dinner at Redmonds, and at McCambridges on the other side of the Triangle where Young's is now; Gammell's, next door, has taken over this function. Beside Redmond's was Kelly's Electrical with the steps up beside it to the narrow hall door, and Gordon's Hardware on the corner, Gordon's Oil and

Colour Merchant, wholesale and retail chandler.

There were laundries throughout Ranelagh, Prescott's and the Dartry Dye Works, and the Dublin Laundry, Bell Dyers and the Swastika Laundry, and three bookies, two of them owned by P. J. Kilmartin, and cake shops! Fitzsimons and Edward's, where Mario's is, and Blanchardstown Mills and the Monument Creamery and Gerards and even Alex Findlater's on the corner of Elmpark Ave, next to Kelly's which had great buns and cakes. And the Kylemore.

The Dublin Laundry and Dartry Dye Works were, incidentally, on the Dodder at the Nine Arches and Orwell Park respectively, and the Swastika Laundry was in Ballsbridge with a huge swastika atop its tall chimney which must have caused some confusion during the war, and indeed after it.

Ranelagh was still a bit country and it wasn't unknown for cattle to run amok on the main road escaping from the small abattoir off Ashfield Avenue. The abattoir served the butchers on Ranelagh where the video store and internet shop is, next door to Humphrey's which is still there; then Clarkes, later Lyster's, then O'Brien's, and now Smiths; and beside that was Keighron's newsagents and when Paddy O'Sullivan took over Lily's Dairy from his mother, and Brian Keighron took over Keighron's from his mother, between the two of them they had Ranelagh surrounded and could give you all the scuttle-butt on just about anything you needed to know. Brian probably still can.

He was at no. 73 Ranelagh and across Ashfield Avenue in front of the long overgrown garden of no. 65 where the Misses Gregg lived in darkened Edwardian splendour (where Tribeca is now) was the bus shelter with a large clock where, if the bus was early, it would wait until its appointed time then the conductors would clock in with their time cards, leaving a confetti of punched-out circles all over the floor and, with a wave to the driver to move off, they'd swing onto the back platform of the already accelerating bus and away off into town.

Some Ranelagh shops

Maher's public house, Kilmartin's bookmaker and Eviston's family grocer, c.1940.

Photograph courtesy of James Connolly Heron

Kelly Bros, Victuallers, nos 45 & 46 Ranelagh, c.1940

Photograph courtesy of Mrs Betty Owens

Kelli, at the same location in 2007

Photograph by Daragh Owens

F. Martin & Sons, no. 6 Field's Terrace, Ranelagh, c.1955. Smokers' requisites, including Camels
and Craven A. Note the life-size nurse promoting the Irish Hospitals' Sweepstake.

Photographs courtesy of the Martin family

Austin Martin behind the counter

Maureen, Austin and Frederick Martin
with Vincent and Justin as children

Dillon's Confectionery, 3 Elmpark Villas, Ranelagh, c.1910

Postcard image courtesy of Michael Murphy

Declan Muldoon outside the Spotless Cleaners in the 1950s

Photograph courtesy of the late Michael Stynes

Albert John Morton's shop on Dunville Avenue in the late 1950s, with his father Charles Morton's shop on the right. The whole of the area pictured is now occupied by the famous Morton's supermarket.

Photograph courtesy of Gary Morton

Ranelagh Seeds and Plants, 2005

Photograph by Garry Murphy

Keegan's Fishmonger & Greengrocer,
Ranelagh, 2001

Photograph by Garry Murphy

Mooney's, no. 32 Dunville Avenue –2004, was a pork butchers, now a pharmacist.

Photograph by Garry Murphy

O'Neill's Fashion Shoe Repairs, no. 38 Dunville Avenue, 2004

Photograph by Garry Murphy

Dowling's, no. 2 Ranelagh, 2008 – shoe repairs while you waited.

Photograph by Daragh Owens

McCarthy's Shoe Shop, Ranelagh, 2008

Photograph by Daragh Owens

The Orchard, Sandford Road, 2008

Photograph by Daragh Owens

Oakline, Ranelagh, 2008

Photograph by Daragh Owens

Ranelagh Multi-denominational School

The school, designed by O'Donnell & Tuomey Architects, was awarded the Royal Institute of Architects in Ireland (RIAI) triennial gold medal in 2005 for the best building completed in Ireland during the period 1998–2000. The school was designed in consultation with local residents and conservation groups and is a wonderful example of how a modern, well-designed functional building can be incorporated into an established historic area. The yellow brick exterior of the building is particularly sensitive to the colour and character of the surrounding Georgian terraces of Old Mountpleasant and Mountpleasant Square. The original eight-classroom school has recently been extended.

Photograph by Ross Galbraith

Ranelagh Heads Exhibition at the Angle, Ranelagh, during Ranelagh Arts Festival, September 2007. *Photograph by Kate Horgan*

Ranelagh Heads Exhibition *by Brigid Tiernan*

The idea for the Exhibition was one I had been thinking about for a while. Firstly as a photographer I was interested in the idea of showing work in the open air. I felt the Angle in Ranelagh was a perfect place to do this and that during the Arts Festival was the time to do it. Secondly, along with outdoor performances I felt that the Exhibition would continue to help bring the Festival out to the people of Ranelagh and others.

As a resident of Ranelagh since 1979, I have seen many changes. The most striking was that there were only two or three other families living on our road when we first moved here. Today, nearly every house is lived in by one family. This didn't just happen by chance. Certain people living in Ranelagh for many years were responsible for this. Others were responsible for the vibrancy of the commercial life of Ranelagh, much of which has since disappeared and been replaced by newer concerns. It seemed to me that very little attention had been given to these older people who were in fact the backbone of Ranelagh. They were ordinary people who had been working away quietly ensuring it would remain a community. If you like, by showing these people to the newer residents of Ranelagh, the Exhibition would continue to reinforce Ranelagh as a community.

I decided then to take photographs of ten older residents and provide a brief biography of their lives in Ranelagh. I know there are, and were, many others who could have been included but I had to start and finish somewhere. In the beginning I began taking photographs of them in their homes but because I wanted the viewer to walk around them and engage with them and the brief description of their lives the images needed to be large and effective. As the work went on it seemed a better idea to take head shots and call the Exhibition 'Ranelagh Heads' having the *double entendre* of long-standing members of the community.

Photograph by Brigid Tiernan

ROSE DOHERTY is 76. At seventeen she came from Baltinglass, Co. Wicklow to work as an assistant cook in Muckross Convent in Marlborough Road. She stayed there for five years and then moved on to the Marist Fathers in Leeson Street where she met her husband Anthony. He was the sacristan there. They married and settled in Ranelagh Avenue where she still lives today. They had four children (one of whom is the snooker champion Ken). Her husband died when the children were young and Rose continued working as a cook in Trinity Hall. She is regularly seen walking her grandchild and on her bike going for messages and doing things for her neighbours and others who may not be feeling too well.

Photograph by Brigid Tiernan

BRIGID DOYLE is 86. Originally from Mullingar, she came to Donnybrook to care for an elderly widower. She worked there for ten years before she married her late husband Patrick Doyle from Ballsbridge. They moved into a cottage in Colliers Avenue where she still lives 49 years later. Her husband Patrick worked for Cantrell & Cochrane. She worked in the home looking after their son and daughter. 'It was easy to do this in Ranelagh, you hadn't a car but it didn't matter because the schools were nearby and the shops sold everything you needed. There was a corner shop and Sandford Cinema at the end of the avenue. Wong's is there now.' Brigid said she loves Ranelagh as much now as when she first came. Her children are well grown, and she has grandchildren, she has a dog and loves feeding the troop of cats that come to her door.

Photograph by Brigid Tiernan

PAULINE FOY is 79. She came to live in Ranelagh after she married Robert Foy in 1961 and has been actively involved in the community ever since. As a mother of two young children she was able 'to open the door and let them and the dog out to play until they came home hungry for dinner'. She became a long time member of the Beechwood Residents Association in an effort to prevent houses being subdivided into flats. They were successful and families began returning to the area in the 1990s. Pauline was a Board member of the Ranelagh Credit Union. She believed in this organisation as she saw how difficult it was for the ordinary citizen, in the 1960s, 1970s and 1980s to borrow money to pay for any extra needs that might have arisen.

Photograph by Brigid Tiernan

BRIAN KEIGHRON is 69 and has lived in Ranelagh since he was three. In the early 1950s his then recently widowed mother bought the shop that became Keighron's Newsagents (now GMale) and Brian began working in the shop fulltime when he left school. He and his wife Olivia had four children. The family continued to run the business until Brian sold it in 2006. The shop was at its busiest in the 1970s and 1980s due to the large number of flats in the area. The nature of life and trading in the village was different then than today. In the 1950s, for example, there were ten newsagents and tobacconists. With no supermarkets it was possible for many small shops to survive. Brian says 'I have very good memories of dealing with the people and miss all the banter of nearly fifty years' trading in Ranelagh.'

Photograph by Brigid Tiernan

IRIS MORTON is 75. She was born in her family home in Sallymount Gardens and was christened and married in the late 1950s in Sandford Church. In fact, 'I came back from my honeymoon on a Sunday, did the washing on Monday and began working in Albert, my late husband's business, on Tuesday. I have worked there happily every since.' At first Morton's Supermarket, in Dunville Avenue, was a small corner general grocery store. Her parents-in-law had a fish shop a few doors away. Over the years the families bought the adjoining buildings and turned it into what it is today. The eldest of her four children, Gary, now runs the business.

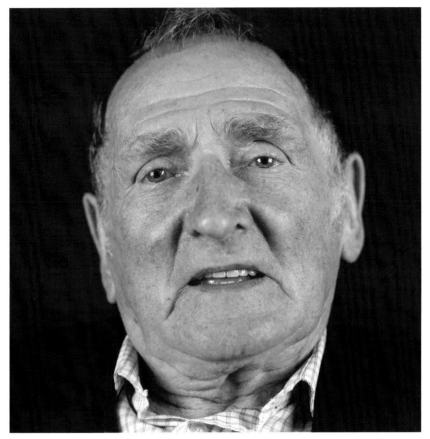

Photograph by Brigid Tiernan

JODIE MCGHEE is 79. He is the second eldest of 14 children, all but one still alive. He was born and brought up in Mountpleasant Buildings (the Buildings were demolished in the 1980s and replaced by Swan Grove). He has spent most of his life in Ranelagh. Jodie served his apprenticeship as a wood machinist for Frank Kenny who ran a furniture company in Harcourt Road supplying government, school and church furniture. He worked there for 39 years. He loved soccer and played many games against local opposition with a team from 'the Buildings'. 'There were so many children in the Buildings in their heyday it was possible to make up a number of soccer teams.'

Photograph by Brigid Tiernan

LIAM O'HAGAN is 71. His parents, Liam and two brothers lived over their grocery store in no. 87 Ranelagh. When he left school in 1956 Liam began working in the shop which had then been expanded into next door. By the 1970s he was joined by his brother Joe. Liam was later to buy no. 83 so the business could include a florist's which was then run by his wife Ann. The business was finally sold in 2002—63 years after it first opened its doors. Liam's early memories of living in the area are of the sound of trams and dray hourses delivering bread and milk to his parents' and other shops close by.

Photograph by Brigid Tiernan

ITA QUILLIGAN was born in 39 Belgrave Square in 1920. Her family have lived there since 1916. She went to school in Scoil Bhríde and Loreto on the Green and then studied art in the National College of Art and Design, She worked as an artist before she married in the early 1940s. She had a large family of 11 children many of whom are also involved in the arts and live in the area. Ita continues to paint and wood carve for which she has a special love. She has had a number of solo exhibitions and also ran children's painting classes in her attic studio for many years.

Photograph by Brigid Tiernan

BRIGID QUINN is 87. She comes from Croghanhill in Co. Offaly but moved to Ranelagh 52 years ago when she married her late husband Tom. He owned Quinn's Hardware shop and when he died suddenly in the early 1960s Brigid had to take over the business while rearing their six children. She was so successful that she was able to put her five daughters and her son through school in the days before free education. At one point three generations of women worked in the shop when her daughter Ann and later granddaughter Karen joined the business. Unfortunately, it closed in the 1990s after half a century trading. In the 1940s, when Quinn's started, Ranelagh had five hardware shops.

Photograph by Brigid Tiernan

MICHAEL STYNES was born in no. 5 Westmoreland Park, Ranelagh in 1939. Sadly, he died in March 2009. He moved away from Ranelagh to Highfield Grove when he was five but he always wanted to come back. It was only in more recent times that he succeeded. In the meantime, he was involved in athletics and training. He was asked to train a group of 50 women who ran under the Belgrave Square banner in the first Women's Mini Marathon in the early 1980s. He swam in the Forty Foot all year round, and as an avid cyclist, he was one of the early campaigners for cycle lanes. He also had a great interest in local history and photography. From early childhood his great interest was soccer and in latter years he regularly trained with the Leinster rugby team playing tennis football, a game he invented, which had the same rules as tennis, played on a tennis court and net over which the ball was headed or kicked. He was a great ideas man for the Ranelagh Arts Festival and will be missed seen cycling and chatting to people in the streets of Ranelagh.

Ranelagh Arts Festival 2005–2008

The following section contains a selection of photographs from various events held during the festival over the past four years, arranged more or less in chronological order.

Ranelagh Arts Festival programmes, 2005–2008

Ranelagh Arts Festival Committee, 2005

(Back, left to right) Ronan O'Donnell, Niall Woods, Robbie Foy, Padraic Ferry, Richard Barrett, Eibhlis Connaughton, Rajbir Gosal, Katherine Johnson, Chloe O'Connor, Helen Kane, Anne O'Donnell

(Front, left to right) Mello Bleahan, Martina Quinn, Deirdre McIntyre, Sheila Griffin, Terry Connaughton

Photograph by Kate Horgan

The Octodeciad, directed by Brendan Ellis, 2005

LEFT TO RIGHT John Healy, Michael O'Donnell, Anne Marie Sheridan, Eibhlis Connaughton

Photographs by Susan Roundtree

RIGHT Donal O'Kelly(left) and Brendan Ellis

ABOVE Kate Horgan and Ken Doherty, 2006. The original print of the photograph by Kate Horgan of Ken Doherty is on permanent display in McSorley's pub in Ranelagh.

Photograph by Daragh Owens

ABOVE Audience at Ranelagh Gardens, 2005

LEFT Seán Gormley performing in Ranelagh Gardens, 2005

RIGHT Ciarán Tourish, Seán Potts and Paul Brady—jigs, reels and tunes, 2006

Photographs by Daragh Owens

LEFT The Cullenswood Singers in the company of the DSO Chamber Group and Charles Pearson present 'An Evening with Mozart', Sandford Parish Church, 2006

Photograph by Kate Horgan

LEFT Henry McCullough,
The Green Beat, 2006

Photograph by Daragh Owens

LEFT Cast of *Thirst*: (back, left to right)
Brendan Ellis, Des Ellis, Seán Gormley,
Finbar Byrne and (front) Friedhelm Arntz,
2006

Photograph by Daragh Owens

RIGHT Zhang Ning (Andy)
and Terry Connaughton,
Karaoke Night, 2006

Photograph by Daragh Owens

ABOVE Terry Connaughton, Ken Doherty, Ciarán Tourish and Gary Morton, 2006

Photograph by Daragh Owens

ABOVE AND LEFT
The Fanzini Brothers at the
Angle, 2007

Photographs by Kate Horgan

RIGHT AND OPPOSITE
Open Day, Ranelagh Gardens,
2007

Photographs by Kate Horgan

Open Day Parade from Scoil Bhríde to Ranelagh Gardens, 2007

Photographs this page by Kate Horgan

Photographs this page by Ross Galbraith

ABOVE Dr Garret FitzGerald opening the History of Ranelagh in Photographs Exhibition in 2007

LEFT Miriam Leech and Daragh Owens at the opening of the History of Ranelagh in Photographs Exhibition, 2007

BELOW Gary Morton, David Lowther, Brigid Tiernan and Sarah Coyle at the opening of the History of Ranelagh in Photographs Exhibition, 2007

Photographs by Kate Horgan

ABOVE Aidan Kelly and Greg Collins, two wonderful friends and supporters of the Ranelagh Arts Festival, gone but not forgotten

Photograph by Kate Horgan

LEFT Anthony Cronin,
Ranelagh Arts Festival, 2007

Photograph by Daragh Owens

RIGHT Mary Stokes performing at the
Ranelagh Arts Festival, 2007

Photograph by Daragh Owens

LEFT Dermot McLaughlin, Ciarán Tourish

BELOW (Left to right) Mark Kelly, Dermot Byrne, Máiréad Ní Mhaonaigh, Ciarán Tourish, Jim Higgins, Ciarán Curran

Photographs by Kate Horgan

LEFT Sally Corcoran leading one of the historical walking tours of Ranelagh, 2007

Photograph by Susan Roundtree

RIGHT Bryan O'Sullivan leading one of the historical walking tours of Ranelagh, 2007
Photograph by Susan Roundtree

ABOVE Detail of the Hornsby Ackroyd 'hot bulb' engine, 2008

Photograph by Daragh Owens

LEFT Fiacc O Brolchain with the restored Hornsby Ackroyd engine at the Angle, Ranelagh, 2008

Photograph by Susan Roundtree

BELOW Fans of the Hornsby Ackroyd engine at the Angle, 2008

Photograph courtesy of Ranelagh Arts Festival

UNDER MILK WOOD

A reading of *Under Milk Wood* by Dylan Thomas took place in Sandford Church during the 2008 Ranelagh Arts Festival, with the support of the Reverend Sonia Gyles and her parishioners. The reading was directed by Brendan Ellis. Janice Williams and Elliw Gwawr guided the pronunciation of the Welsh words. Those taking part were: (back row, left to right) David Heap, Fintan Lawlor, John Coll, Bart Felle, Edward O'Hare, Tony Farmar, Breeda Connaughton, Maeve Carton, Anna Farmar (hidden), Macdara Woods, Jenny Robinson, Andrew Robinson, John McCarthy, Colin Boyle, Keith Brennan, Val Roche, Dermot Carmody, John Stanton, Fiacc O Brolchain, Rachel McNicholl, Jim Lockhart, Aidan White, Donal O'Kelly, Mick McNally, John Keogh, Anna O'Hare, (middle row, standing, left to right) Gráinne Arntz, Sorcha Fox, Katherine Farmar, Áine Nich Giolla Choille, Emer O'Connell, Sonia Gyles, Kate Horgan, Sean Gormley, Honor O Brolchain, Michelle D'Arcy, Susan Roundtree, Mick Halpenny, Yvonne Twohey, Anne-Marie Sheridan, Caroline Walsh, Bettina Peters, Maureen Rafter, (middle row, seated, left to right) Ross Galbraith, Janice Williams, Eiléan Ní Chuileanáin, Isolde Carmody, John Healy, Brenda Wilkes, (front, on the floor) Brendan Ellis, Nollaig Rowan, Barbara Coll. Also included are the guide dogs Wilma and Quazi.

Photograph by Kate Horgan

RIGHT Councillor Mary Freehill, Rose Doherty and Frank McNally unveiling the commemorative sculpture to honour Richard Crosbie in Ranelagh Gardens, 2008

Photograph by Daragh Owens

LEFT Descendents of Richard Crosbie with Councillor Mary Freehill at the unveiling of his commemorative sculpture in Ranelagh Gardens, 2008. (Back, left to right) Eleanor Lamb, Fionnbarr McDermott Long, Deirdre McDermott, (front) Helen Lamb

Photograph by Daragh Owens

ABOVE A Taste of Ranelagh Art, 2008, featured the work of local artists including (back, left to right) Caroline Canning, Cian McLoughlin, Yoko Akino, Áine Clinton, Michael Bulfin, Mark Ryan, (front, left to right) Marie Hennessy, Mello Bleahan, Rosemary McLoughlin, Imelda Healy

Photograph by Daragh Owens

SELECT BIBLIOGRAPHY

Bourke, Angela *Maeve Brennan: Homesick in New York*
London, 2005

Clare, J., O'Connell, M., Simmons, A. (eds) *The Culwick
Choral Society celebrates one hundred years 1898–1998*
Dublin, 1998

Daly, Mary, Peter Pearson and Mona Hearn *Dublin's
Victorian Houses* Dublin, 1998

de Courcy, John W. & Sheila *Church of the Holy Name,
History & Guide* (pamphlet) 1996

Dublin City Council *The Georgian Squares of Dublin*
Dublin, 2006

Ferguson, Paul (ed.) *The A to Z of Georgian Dublin, John
Rocque's maps of the City in 1756 and the County in 1760*
Lympne Castle, Kent, 1998

Hickey, Kieran *The Light of Other Days, Irish Life at the
Turn of the Century in the Photographs of Robert French*
London, 1973

Igoe, Vivien *A Literary Guide to Dublin* London, 1999

Kelly, Deirdre *Four Roads to Dublin: A History of
Rathmines, Ranelagh, and Leeson Street* Dublin, 1995

Mac Aongusa, Brian *The Harcourt Street Line: Back on
Track* Dublin, 2003

O Brolchain, Honor *All in the Blood* Dublin, 2006

O'Donnell, E. E. *Father Browne's Dublin: Photographs
1925–1950* Dublin, 1996

O'Maitiu, Seamus *Dublin's Suburban Towns 1834–1930*
Dublin, 2003

Simms, Dr J. G. & James, Dermot *Sandford Church
1826–1976*, (pamphlet) 1976

Sisson, Elaine *Pearse's Patriots: St Enda's and the Cult of
Boyhood* Cork, 2004

Sweeney, Clair L. *The Rivers of Dublin* Dublin, 1991

INDEX OF NAMES